£1.99
'98

GW01087137

A Trevor Wye

Practice Book for the

Flute

Volume

Breathing and Scales

Order No: NOV 120588

NOVELLO PUBLISHING LIMITED
8/9 Frith Street, London W1V 5TZ

© Copyright 1985 Novello & Company Limited

Reprinted 1986

Reprinted (with revisions) 1990, 1994

All Rights Reserved

No part of this publication may be copied or
reproduced in any form or by any means
without the prior permission of Novello &
Company Limited.

For PETER-LUKAS GRAF – *with affection*

CONTENTS

		page
BREATHING		
(a)	and your body	5
(b)	and lungevity	8
(c)	and musical phrasing	9
EXPRESSIVE SCALES and ARPEGGIOS		12
TECHNICAL SCALES and ARPEGGIOS		24
SCALES IN THIRDS and BROKEN ARPEGGIOS		33
IMPROVISATION		43
PLAYING FROM MEMORY		53

A PREFACE TO BE READ

TO THE STUDENT

This book is about practising; how to extract the most from it, how to be more efficient at it and how to isolate and overcome some of the difficulties of the flute. It is by no means intended to be definitive. It was written to help you achieve good results with many of the flute problems, in the shortest time.

If the exercises are practised properly, it will shorten the time spent on the building blocks of flute playing, and so allow more time for music making.

These points about practising in general, are important:

(a) Practise the flute only because you *want* to; if you don't want to – don't! It is almost useless to spend your allocated practice time wishing that you weren't practising.

(b) Having *decided* to practise, make it difficult. Like a pest inspector, examine every corner of your tone and technique for flaws and practise to remove them. Only by this method will you improve quickly. After glancing through this book, you will see that many of the exercises are simply a way of looking at the same problem from different angles. You will not find it difficult to invent new ways.

(c) Try always to practise what you *can't* play. Don't indulge in too much self-flattery by playing through what you can already do well.

(d) As many of the exercises are taxing, be sure your posture and hand positions are correct. It is important to consult a good teacher on these points (see page 9 in Practice Book VI—ADVANCED PRACTICE).

GUARANTEE

Possession of this book is no guarantee that you will improve on the flute; there is no magic in the printed paper. But, if you have the desire to play well and put in some reasonable practice, you cannot fail to improve. It is simply a question of *time*, *patience* and *intelligent work*. The book is designed to avoid unnecessary practice. It is concentrated stuff. *Provided* that you follow the instructions carefully, you should make more than twice the improvement in half the time! *That is the guarantee.*

PREFACE

This is the last of the basic Practice Books and completes a survey of the building blocks of flute playing. Like constructing a house, each brick is dependent upon another; a weakness in the early stages will cause problems later. Each of these Books has a dependence upon the others. All are aimed toward the same end: TO ENABLE YOU TO LEARN THE FLUTE THOROUGHLY IN THE SHORTEST TIME. This makes it possible to spend more time on pieces, less on exercises and, perhaps, more time at the beach.

Practice Book 6 – An Advanced Practice Book – is concerned with advanced exercises based on the material contained in the first five books.

It's all a question of . . . . , ... , and . . . . !

T.W. 1984

BREATHING
BREATHING AND YOUR BODY

Firstly, assuming that you have survived to read this sentence, there really can't be much wrong with the way you breathe, though to play a few notes on a pipe as the ancients did is simple; the requirements of modern flute playing, of composers, and therefore of the musical phrase, demand that more detailed attention be paid to the way we breathe.

What is curious is that we breathe most naturally when horizontal; this is our most relaxed position. Any breathing difficulties are experienced when standing upright.

Wind players need lots of air in their lungs and they need the utmost control over its intake and expulsion. The flute player uses more air than any other wood-wind player; for that reason alone it is necessary to ensure that this basic process is correctly learned.

It is not proposed here to go into the medical mechanics of taking and expelling breath, which could be misleading, confusing, unhelpful and even downright daft. You don't need to know all the precise mechanical processes taking place in a car in order to drive one. A fully explanatory article (of which there are many) with copious, revolting, medical diagrams should be read by the dead who have a desperate need to know of such matters, or by the insatiably curious living. Here we will confine ourselves to an examination only of what is strictly necessary for flute playing.

Of the many opinions about breathing, one clear point emerges, namely that it is wrong to raise the shoulders when taking in a breath. The reasons will become clearer when you start the exercises. It is wrong because (a) it tightens the throat and often leads to (b) a bleating, goat-like vibrato (see Practice Book 4, Page 22) which, in turn usually (c) encourages the development of grunts, or vocal cord noises, whilst playing. Raising the shoulders also (d) makes it impossible to properly control the expulsion of air from the lungs and (e) it conflicts with the way in which the flute tone should develop with regard to the mouth and throat cavities (see TONE in Practice Book 6).

In short, don't.

The rib cage contains the lungs. The rib bones are fastened to the spine at the back, and to the breast bone in front. The breast bone divides into two branches half way down your front. Because of this division, the lower ribs are able to expand to some extent; the upper ones less so, though due to the softness and flexibility of bones and tissues, they have some outward movement. Underneath both lungs is a membrane, not unlike a muscular drum skin, called the *diaphragm*. The muscles of the diaphragm can be tightened or relaxed. When tightened, the diaphragm flattens; when it relaxes, it resumes its natural position which is dome-shaped in an upward direction. Muscles can only work in one direction – by contracting. When contracted, the dome-shaped diaphragm flattens and thus draws air into the lungs. The *abdominal muscles* are used to expel the air from the lungs. With your hand on your abdomen you can feel these muscles by tightening them and relaxing them as in coughing, or laughing.
A normal breath involves tightening the diaphragm to pull the lungs downwards; this creates a vacuum in the lungs causing air to rush in through the mouth. *Relaxing* the diaphragm and *tightening* the abdominal muscles will push the diaphragm back into its upwards dome-shape, thus expelling the air.

That is about as much air as is necessary for a big sigh; for flute playing more is needed, which is why some exercises must be done.

EXERCISE I

Place your hand on your abdomen; when breathing in, your abdomen should move out; when breathing out, it should move back in.* You should become thinner when breathing out, and fatter when breathing in.

Now place your hands on your hips but reverse your hand position so that the outside, or back, of the wrists is against your pelvic bone with the palms of the hands facing outwards. Now take a breath as before pushing the abdomen outwards but this time continuing to take in air by *expanding the rib cage sideways.*

You become *wider*, not *taller*. These diagrams may help you understand.

Let's assume the lungs are like a box:—

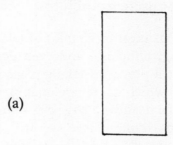

(a)

When a gentle breath is taken in, the lower part expands:—

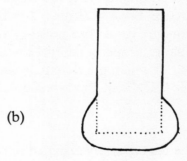

(b)

When a large breath is taken in, with the rib-cage expanding sideways, it would look like:—

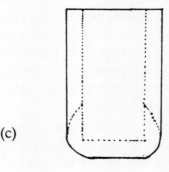

(c)

*If you have any difficulty experiencing this, sit in an upright chair, fold your body forward until your hands touch the ground and your abdomen is resting on your thighs. Breathe in and raise yourself slightly as you do so. You should feel the pressure of your abdomen on your thighs. *Or* lie flat on the floor. Place a book on your abdomen, gently breathe in and out raising the book when breathing *in*.

If the shoulders were raised, it would look like:—

(d)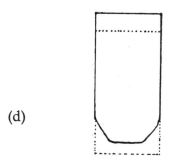

Observe how the abdomen becomes thinner when the shoulders are raised.

So far, this should be quite straightforward. Unfortunately, the position in which the flute is held tends to encourage shoulder-breathing, especially for beginners who, in their first few weeks, attempt to support the head-joint with the left shoulder.*

Look in a mirror. Is your rib cage going upwards when breathing in? It shouldn't be. Are you raising your shoulders?

Just to check: with your hands hanging by your sides, (a) take a deep breath deliberately raising the shoulders and holding your abdomen in, (b) place your wrists on your hips and repeat the breath, expanding first your abdomen and secondly, your rib cage. See the difference?

Take up your flute and play long notes checking at each breath that the shoulders are down when breathing in, and the throat is relaxed. Use a mirror.

Play some pieces and check yourself often. For the proper control of the air supply, Exercise I is sufficient for the time being.

For 'support' of the flute tone and to obtain that singing quality, especially in the third octave, you will need to refer to the Tone Section in Practice Book 6 dealing with abdominal tension, where it is fully explained.

For a *really* large intake of air you will need to practise Exercise II which is set out in the next section, LONGEVITY.

---

*Correct posture is essential to correct breathing, especially the flute/body relationship, and the left hand and arm position (see Beginners' Book for Flute – Novello; also in Practice Book 6).

BREATHING AND LUNGEVITY

Your lungs are capable of expanding far in excess of the size of your chest; the problem is that the ribs prevent them. This section concerns increasing the expansion and contraction of the ribs so that the lungs can accommodate more air. *It's the difference between the expansion and contraction of your ribs which directly affects how long you can play without taking another breath.*

EXERCISE II

Place your hands backwards on your hips. Start by breathing out all the air in your lungs. *All* the air, not just most of it. Yes, really; *all* of it! It *should* feel uncomfortable. Now breathe in slowly through your nose. Start filling the abdomen first then expand the ribs outwards. You may also feel your back filling out. Take in the *maximum* that you can. *Do not breathe out:* now take a bit more. *Yes you can!* and a bit more, *and a bit more still.* Hold it. Now breathe out slowly. Get rid of every bit of air in your lungs, keep breathing out until it feels painful. Now relax. Begin again. Repeat six times.

The whole exercise cycle feels a little uncomfortable, doesn't it? Your ribs aren't used to such big movements. Ask a friend with a tape measure to measure your capacity. The tape goes around your chest a couple of inches or so below your arm-pits. Expel *all* the air. Take a reading. Take in as much air as possible expanding your ribs. Take another reading. The *difference* between the two readings is your expansion.

Untrained, your expansion is likely to be between one and two inches (2.5 – 5 cms). Write it down on this table:

MONTH	YEAR	EXPANSION
JANUARY		
FEBRUARY		
MARCH		
APRIL		
MAY		
JUNE		
JULY		
AUGUST		
SEPTEMBER		
OCTOBER		
NOVEMBER		
DECEMBER		

If you make about six huge expansions and contractions *several times a day*, you will double your expansion in about a year to 18 months! That may mean no more worrying about long phrases. You should keep this up until your expansion/contraction is around four to five inches (10 – 12.5 cms). It is not the size or your body that counts, though big people do have some advantage; it's the amount by which you *expand and contract* that counts. Even small, thin people can obtain a large difference. It's all a question of

_____, _____ and _____ _____!

Finally, check yourself against a long musical phrase you know well and see whether each week you can last out for a longer time before you have to stop due to lack of breath. Mark your stopping place each day.

About twelve to eighteen months of these exercises should double your expansion, possibly even sooner. You will certainly notice the difference in your performances.

Some more advice about the relationship between the air supply and your tone can be found in Practice Book 6.

BREATHING AND MUSICAL PHRASING

Find a sentence containing commas and semicolons. There are plenty in this book. Notice what they do to a sentence. Notice where you take a breath.

1 They contribute to the *sense* of the sentence
2 They assist in the *forward flow* of the meaning.
3 Your breathing can be part of the way you express the meaning of the writer.

So it is in music.

Breathing marks are not enemies. Yes, they are necessary but they should become part of the expression of music and not a human failing. Prick yourself with a pin. Before you howl in anguish, you breathe in quickly. Think about this. The quickly indrawn breath becomes *part* of your expression of pain. So it is in music.

Breathing in music can't really be explained; the most we can do is provide guidelines. *Breathing, and breathing places, can only be proved by the performance.* There are many opinions on where to breathe. Breathing can *add* to the expression of a musical phrase. *It can also detract from it.*

Consider this phrase from the opening of Fauré's Fantasie:-

FANTASIE

FAURÉ

There are many possibilities for breathing. In bar 2, the bass line is rising and continues to rise into bar 3. This indicates a forward musical movement. It's not *bad* to breathe at (A), simply undesirable. *But,* supposing a slight crescendo is made during bar 2 and continued *right up to* the breath at (A), if then the second note of bar 3 is played *as if the crescendo continues,* then the breath is not only unnoticed, but contributes to the forward motion of the music. If the performer were to make a *diminuendo* to bar three and take the breath at (A), it would halt the forward motion of the phrase. This is what often happens. Breathing, then, can contribute a great deal toward the sense and forward motion of a musical phrase. If a deliberate diminuendo, or announcement, is made that a breath is to be taken, it then interrupts the forward motion.

Back to Fauré. Marked below are a variety of options on where to breathe. They all depend on where you consider the phrase-bits end, or temporarily rest. As mentioned before, breath (A) isn't really good because of the ascending bass line. (B) is not satisfactory as the phrase continues through the bar to the D sharp − E resolution. (C) is good if the natural diminuendo (suspension-resolution of D sharp to E) is continued through the breath into bar five. (D) is the parallel place to (A) and is not good for the same reason. (E) is parallel to (B); there is no natural end to the phrase here. (F) is parallel to (C) and should, logically, be taken. However, because of the natural direction of notes in bar eight, many would prefer the breath at (G). (H) and (I) both sound daft, although if (A) is taken, then perhaps (H) and (I) should be as well. (J) could be taken, though it would interrupt the rising melody. (K) is parallel to (G), (L) is parallel to (A).

The F sharp in bar thirteen has a natural forward motion through bar fourteen on to the surprise F natural at bar fifteen. Therefore (M) isn't good and (N) would ruin the natural phrase-end at (O). (P) is, of course, parallel to (O).

How many other breaths can you find and justify?

The study of this passage leads to a conclusion; although *where* to breathe is important, it is also *how* the breath is taken; *how* it is prepared; *how* the interruption is restarted after the breath.

BREATHING WILL PRESENT FEW PROBLEMS WHEN IT BECOMES VERY IMPORTANT TO YOU TO CONTINUE THE FORWARD FLOW OF THE MUSICAL PHRASE.

Here are some guidelines:—

1) Mark your breathing in where you think it should be in a piece you are playing at the moment. Ask yourself, as a guide:—
   (a) what is the harmony doing?
   (b) what is the bass doing?
   (c) where is the melody going?

2) Don't divide the music up into bite-sized chunks in order to make it look evenly spaced. You can take more than one breath in a bar if you wish, or if you *have* to. Several short breaths can result in a long following phrase which may be more musically satisfying.

3) Practise how to breathe quickly. See below for some exercises.

4) *Use your breathing places to make the music more expressive: breathing then becomes part of your way of expressing the music.*

5) When marking your breathing, look both ahead and behind to the parallel phrases which, as nearly as possible, should correspond; but consider points (1) (a), (b) and (c) above.

6) The note before a breath must not diminuendo or be musically terminated ($\Longrightarrow$) as this announces the breath long before it happens. You wouldn't put in the diminuendo (or Note Ending − see P.B. No. 1) if you were *not* going to breathe.

7) The note before a breath must remain *beautiful* until the breath takes place.

8) The note immediately after a breath must take over where the previous note left off. Much more clever still would be to assume that the crescendo *continues* through the breath and therefore the note after takes over at the crescendo point it *would* have reached had the breath not taken place!

9) The note after a breath must be *more* musical and expressive than the one before the breath.

Here are two exercises to work at:−

1) With your flute, first practise taking a breath in quickly, completely filling the lungs. Do you make a noise when taking in air? If you do this could be caused by:-
   (a) raised shoulders, therefore, a tight throat.
   (b) not opening your mouth wide enough; drop your jaw and with your teeth together, suck in air. It should feel cold on your teeth. Repeat with your teeth further apart; this time the cold air affects the back of your throat. Open your mouth and throat so that the cold feeling is well down in your lungs. Your breathing will also be silent.
   (c) your head is lowered with your chin near your chest. Hold your head up!
   (d) perhaps, just a tight throat.
Test yourself with a piece well-known to you and check the points above.

2) Play the first long note below; as *quickly as possible*, stop, take a breath, and restart your note. Work at shortening the time taken to breathe. You will quickly find that the time taken and the amount of air taken in are directly connected to your ability to open the throat and mouth wide enough.

EXPRESSIVE SCALES AND ARPEGGIOS

These are amongst the most important exercises for experiencing the movement of a beautiful tone through the compass of the flute. Mould your tone to the key you are in. Push the intensity of your tone forward as you ascend; learn to return to your starting point when descending; let each phrase of two bars lead naturally to the next pair. Use your tone to change key (see Practice Book 1, TONE − page 24). These exercises are useful both to study the movement of expression and as daily warm-up exercises.

EXPRESSIVE SCALES

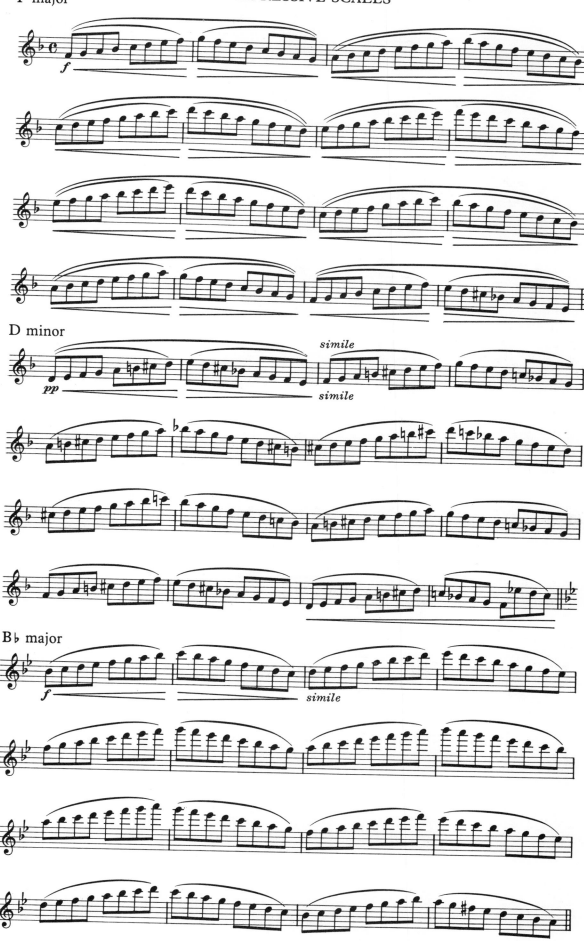

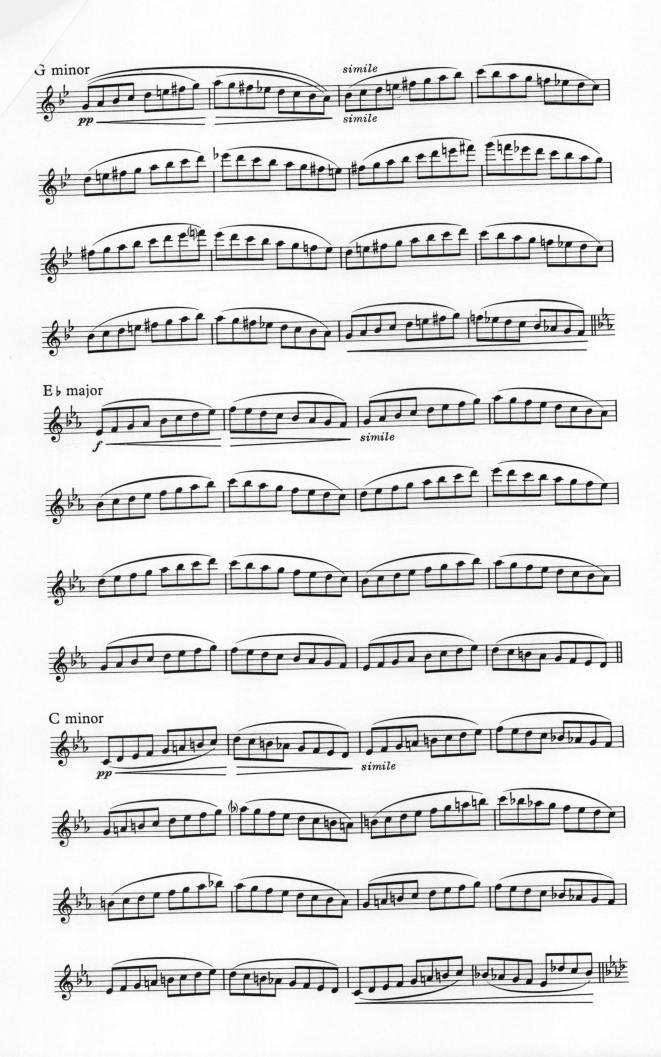

A♭ major

F minor

D♭ major

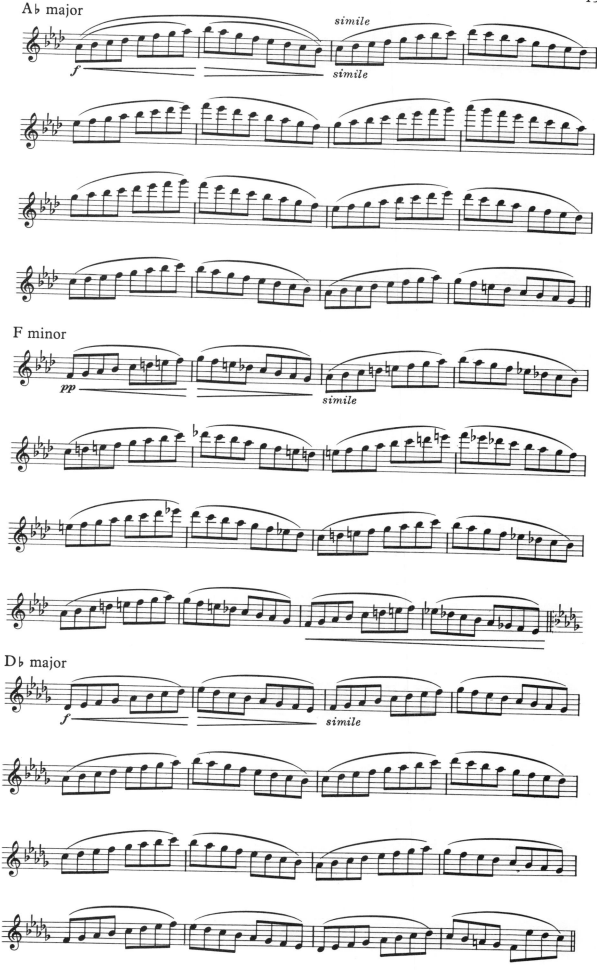

16

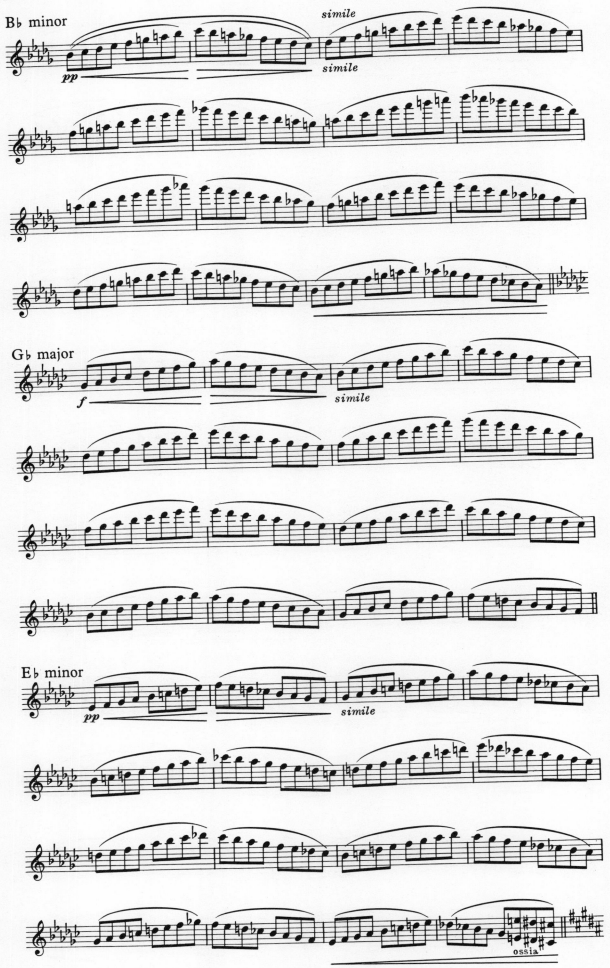

B major

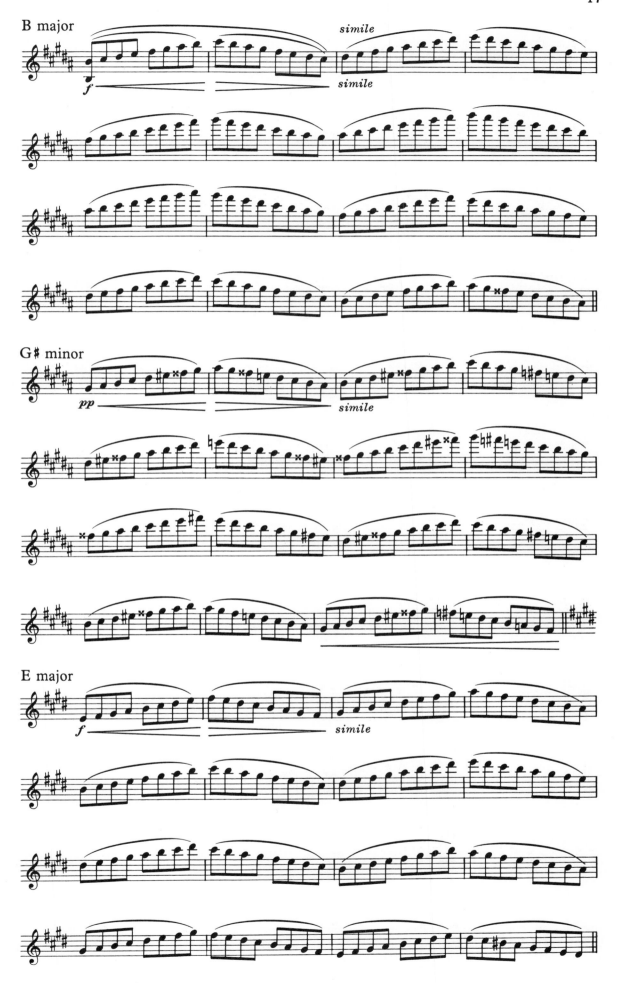

G# minor

E major

18

C# minor

A major

F# minor

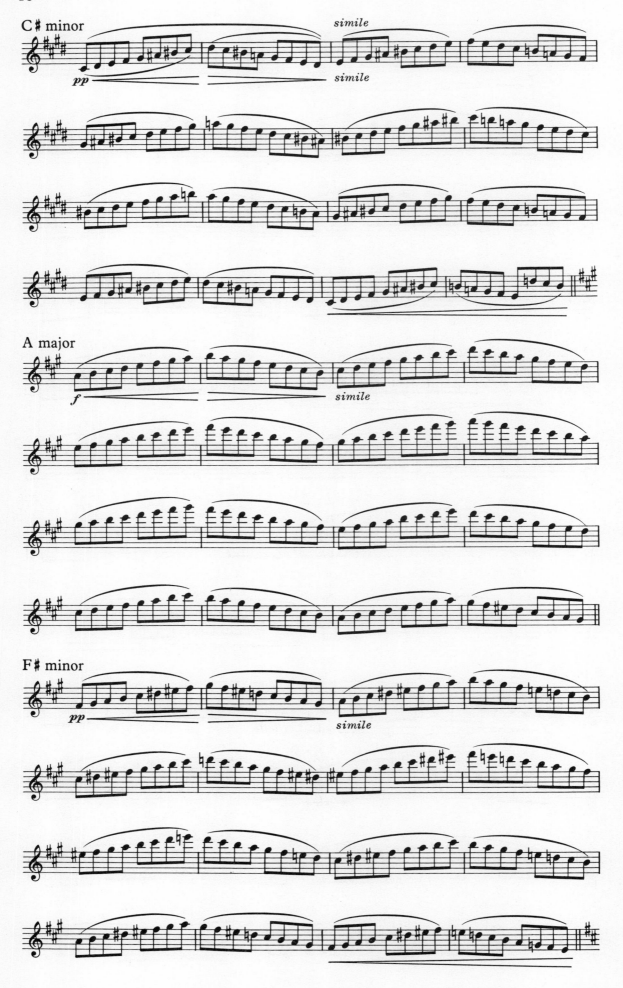

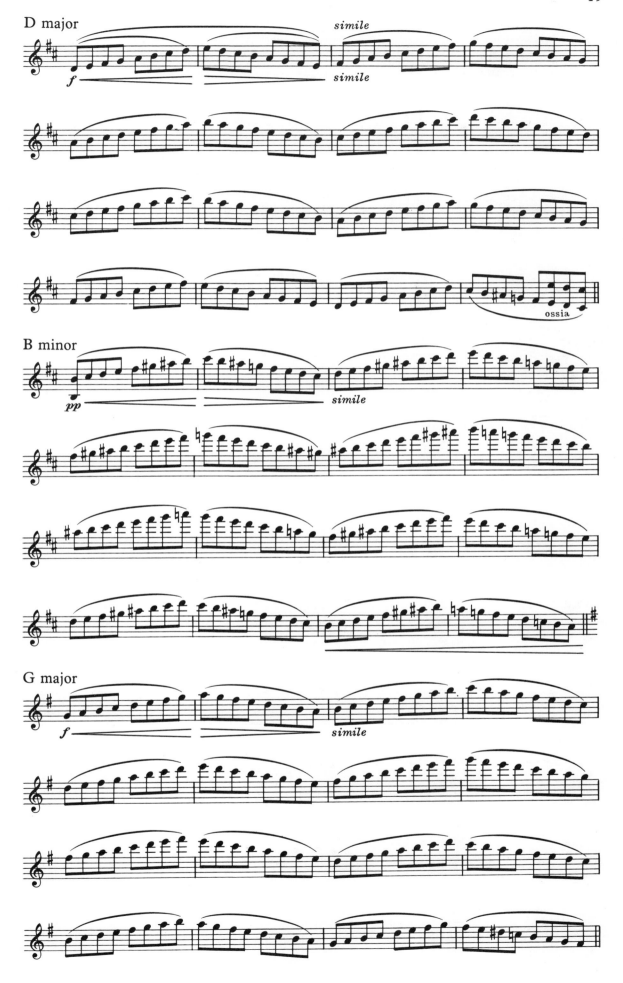

D major

simile

B minor

G major

20

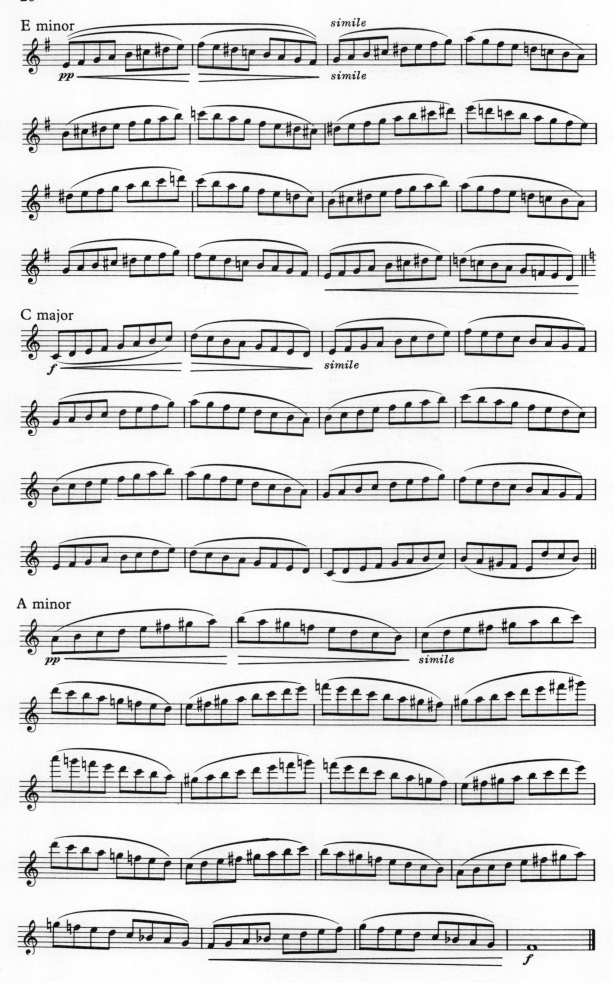

EXPRESSIVE ARPEGGIOS

Practise as in the Expressive Scales.

Learn to make your tone SING.

Feel happy! The weather may be lousy; pretend it isn't.

If you are not enjoying them with the resultant improvement in your tone, you are sick: put your flute in its case and go to bed.

(BUT PRACTISE TWICE TOMORROW!)

PRACTISE THIS ARPEGGIO SECTION IN TWO WAYS:—

Remember Practice Book 3 ARTICULATION, page 9 exercise 6? LOOK IT UP. In 18th century music the slur = diminuendo; don't shorten the second note.

EXPRESSIVE ARPEGGIOS

F major

D minor

B♭ major

G minor

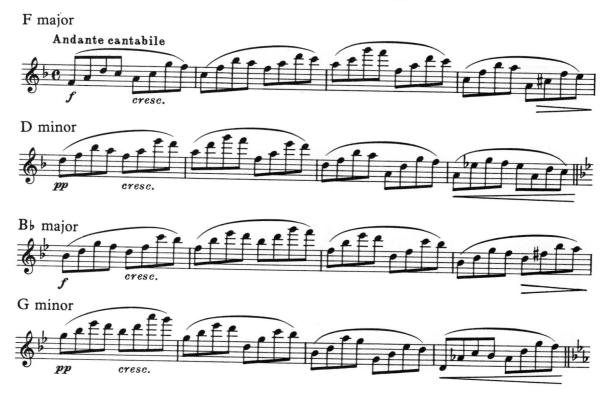

22

Eb major

C minor

Ab major

F minor

Db major

Bb minor

Gb major

Eb minor

B major

G# minor

TECHNICAL SCALES AND ARPEGGIOS
SECTIONS ONE, TWO AND THREE

All the technical exercises in Practice Book 2 – TECHNIQUE – were designed as basic practice material for this next section.

It really is impossible to develop a good technique and to be able to exercise control over your fingers, lips and tongue without scales and arpeggios.

Here are some hints on how to tackle this section:—

(a) Play them through at any convenient speed. If they are really beyond your technical capabilities at this stage then work at Practice Book 2 thoroughly first, especially the third octave.

(b) Always play scales and arpeggios with your *best* tone.

(c) Always play them with the same expressiveness that you used in the previous section; they must sound beautiful.

(d) If the third octave presents any problems, mark the section as a group of twelve notes (to cover all the offending notes) and practise these later for a short time. Every third day, leave the scales and arpeggios and concentrate only on these groups of twelve notes. In this way, they will rapidly improve and will soon equal the lower two octaves.

(e) Mark the keys you find most difficult and practise *only* these every third day.

(f) Read, once again, the Preface to this, and every other Practice Book. Yes, I know you've read it before, but read it again. *This means you!*

SECTION ONE – SCALES:
CHROMATIC, WHOLE TONE, MAJOR AND MINOR

Chromatic scale

Whole tone scales

MAJOR AND MINOR SCALES

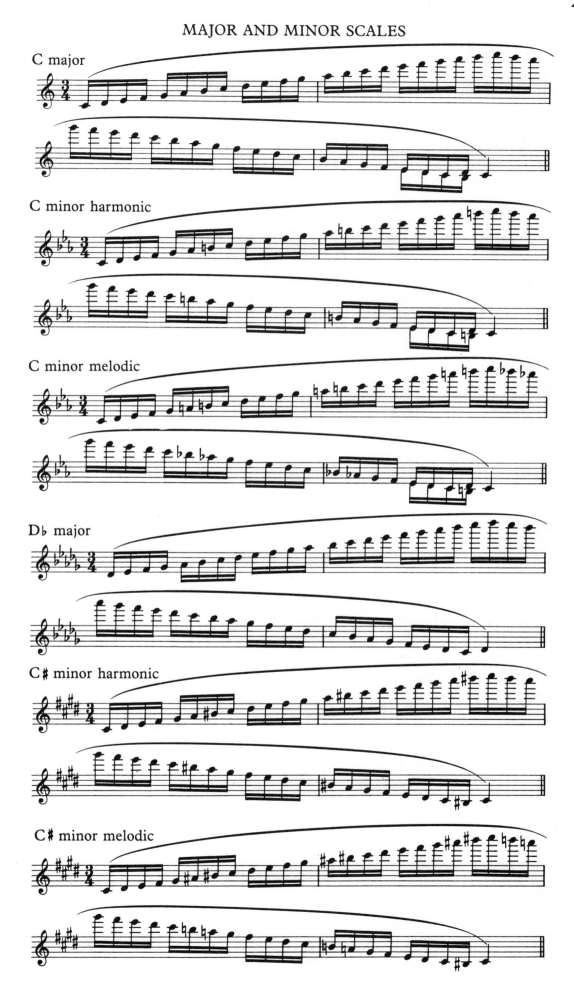

26

D major

D minor harmonic

D minor melodic

E♭ major

E♭ minor harmonic

E♭ minor melodic

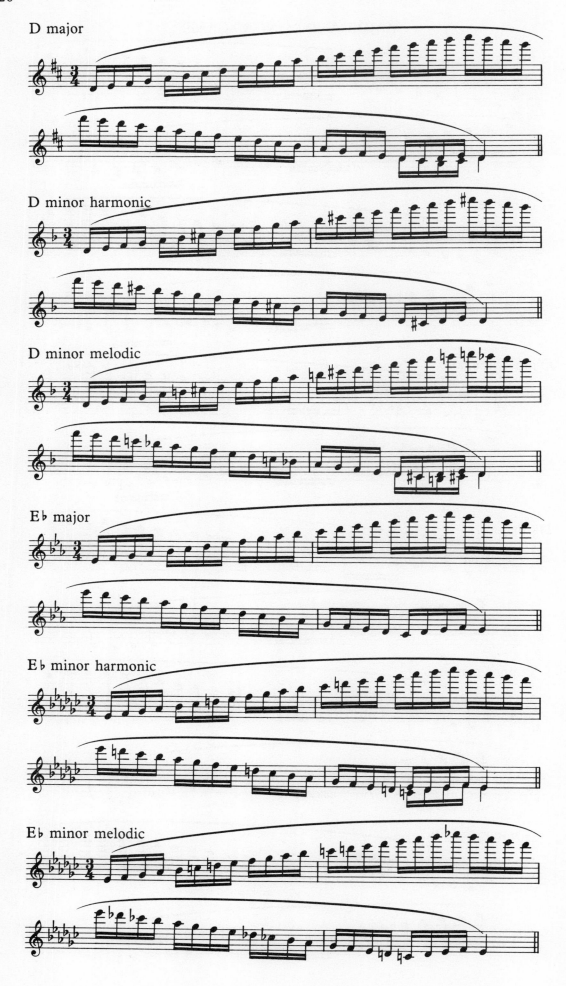

E major

E minor harmonic

E minor melodic

F major

F minor harmonic

F minor melodic

28

F# major

F# minor harmonic

F# minor melodic

G major

G minor harmonic

G minor melodic

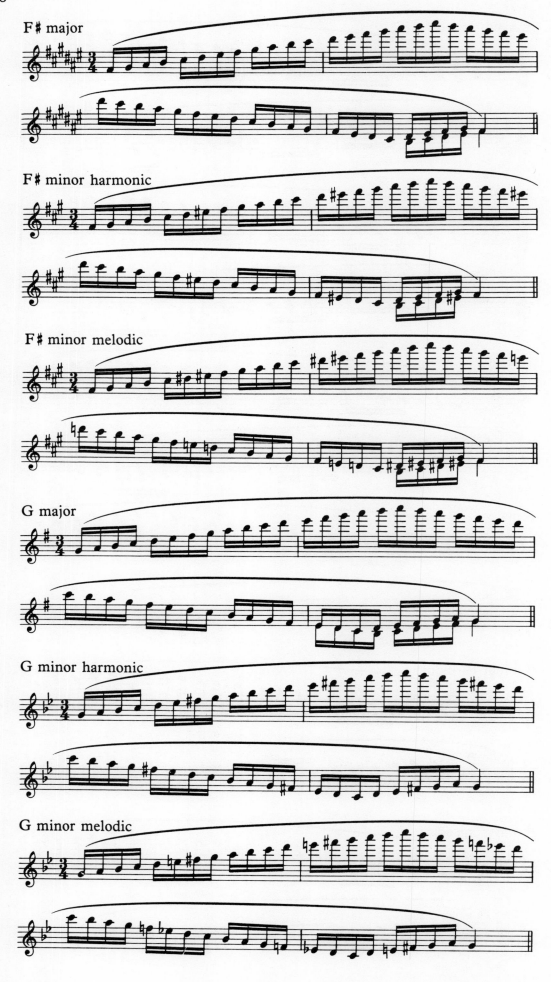

A♭ major

G♯ minor harmonic

G♯ minor melodic

A major

A minor harmonic

A minor melodic

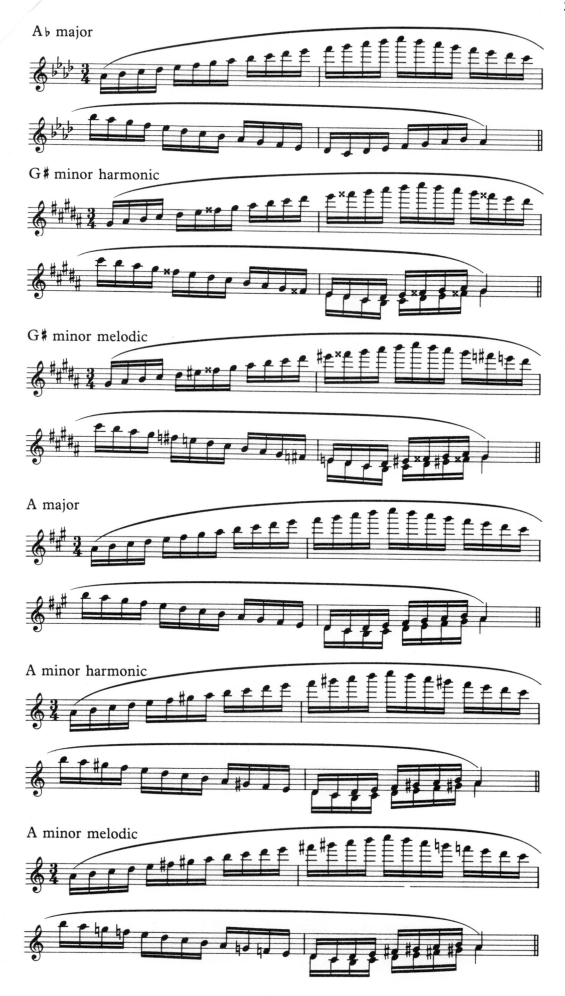

30

Bb major

Bb minor harmonic

Bb minor melodic

B major

B minor harmonic

B minor melodic

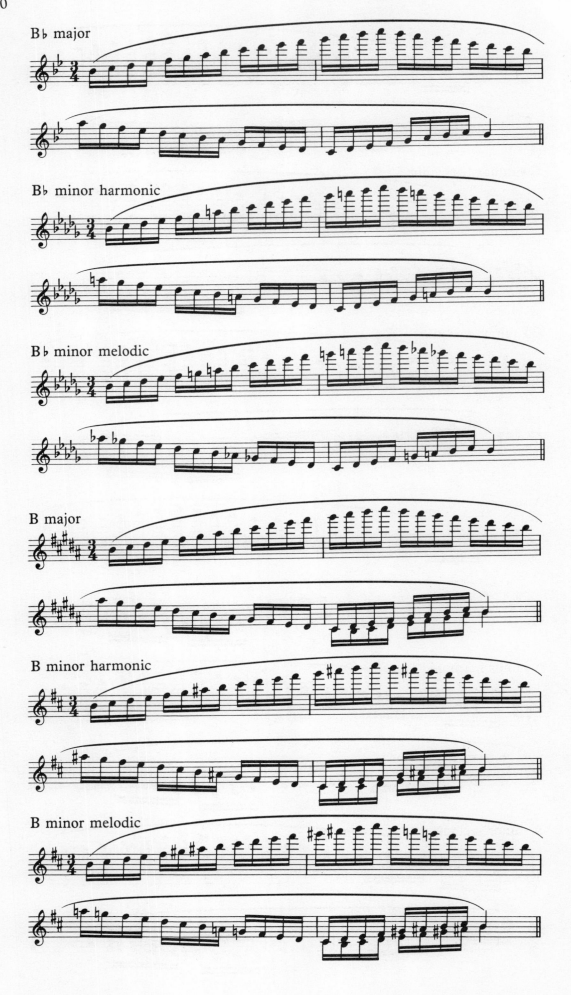

SECTION TWO – ARPEGGIOS: MAJOR, MINOR AND DIMINISHED

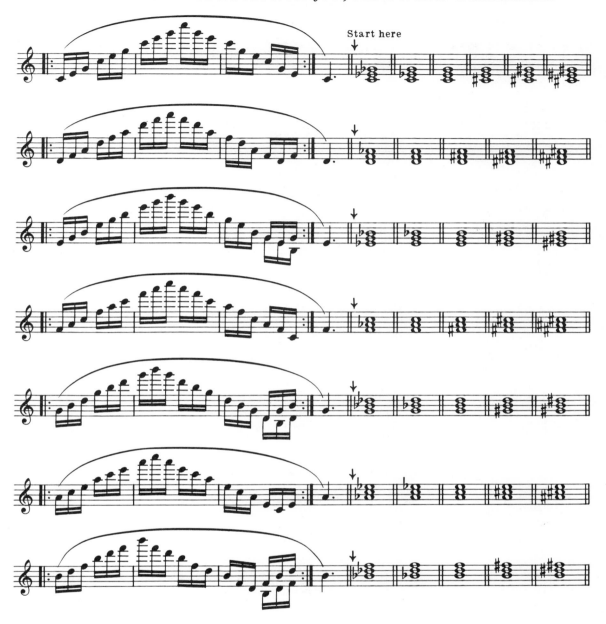

SECTION THREE – DIMINISHED SEVENTH ARPEGGIOS

OTHER ARPEGGIOS OF THE SEVENTH

SECTIONS FOUR, FIVE AND SIX

SCALES IN THIRDS AND BROKEN ARPEGGIOS

These represent the final stage in the acquisition of a basic technique. If you have got so far, nothing must stop you from finishing the job off properly.

By exercising your fingers on these, and the previous scales, you have taught them note patterns which occur in most of the flute literature most of the time. Expressed another way, you have learned 95% of 90% of the entire flute repertoire! Or, you have learned 85.5% of all flute music.

It's time well spent.

So, get to it!

SECTION FOUR – MAJOR SCALES IN THIRDS

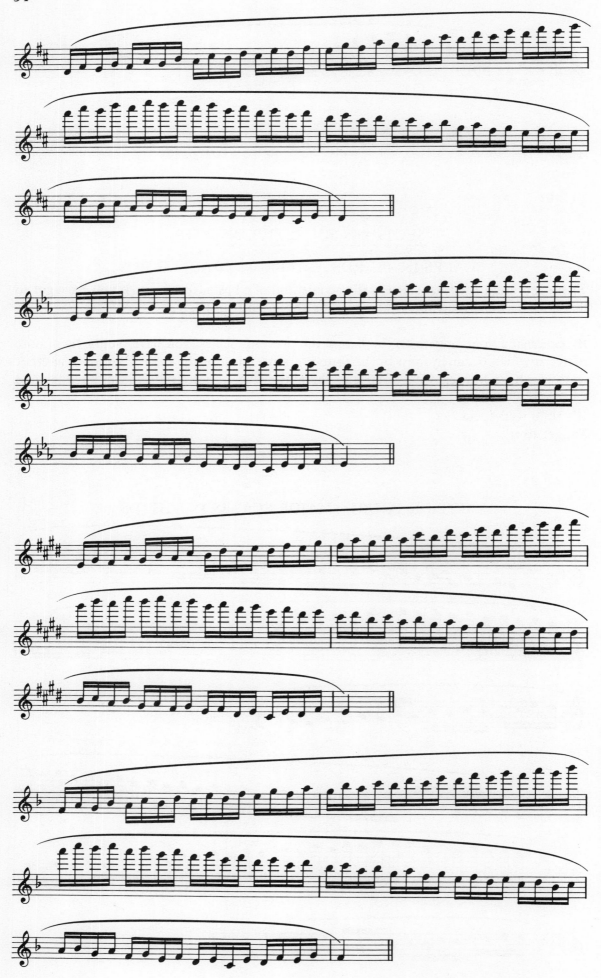

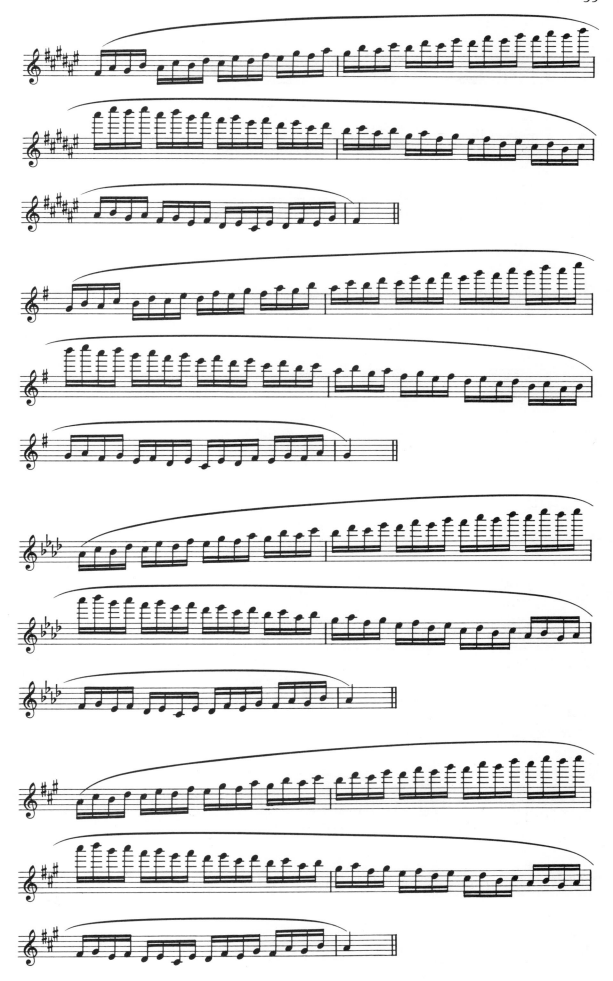

36

MINOR SCALES IN THIRDS

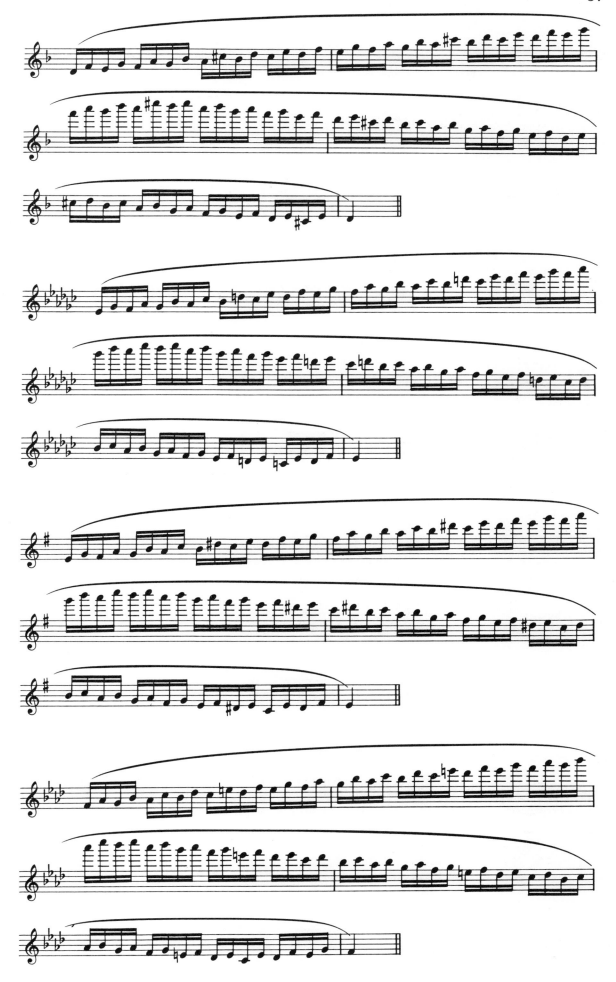

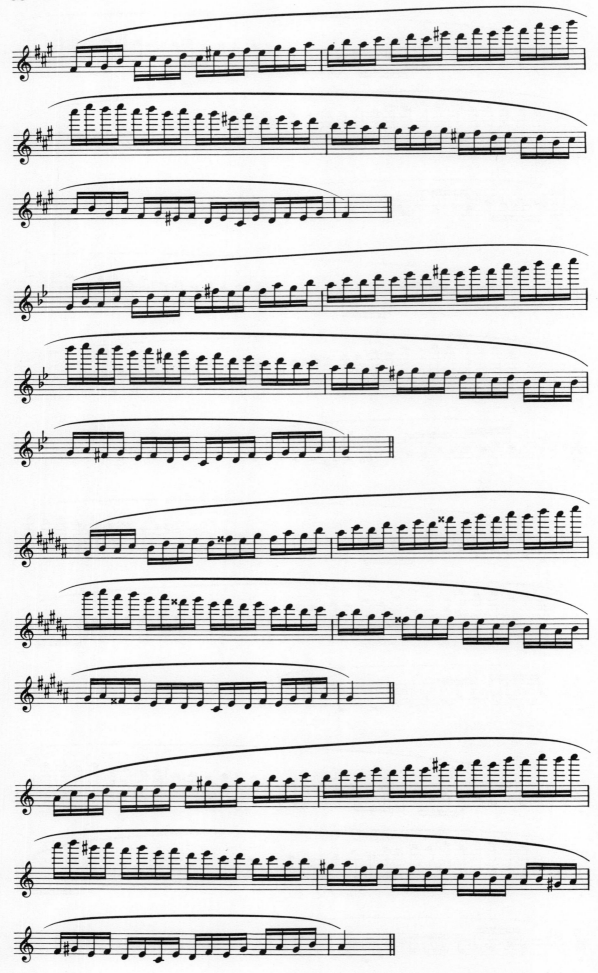

CHROMATIC SCALES

WHOLE TONE SCALES

SECTION FIVE – DIMINISHED ARPEGGIOS

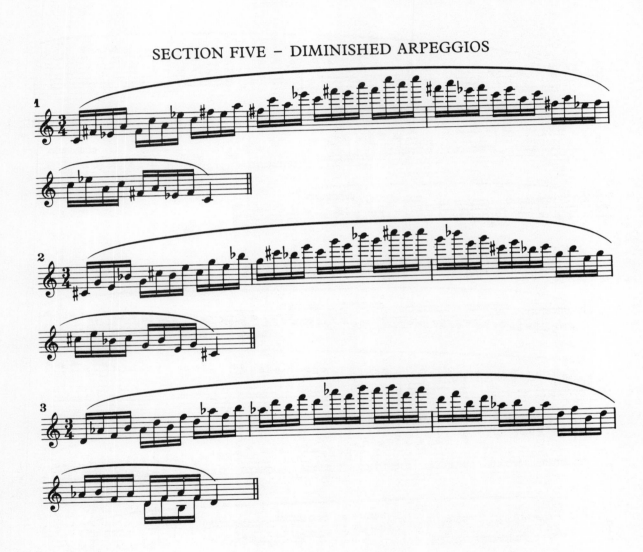

SECTION FIVE – BROKEN ARPEGGIOS

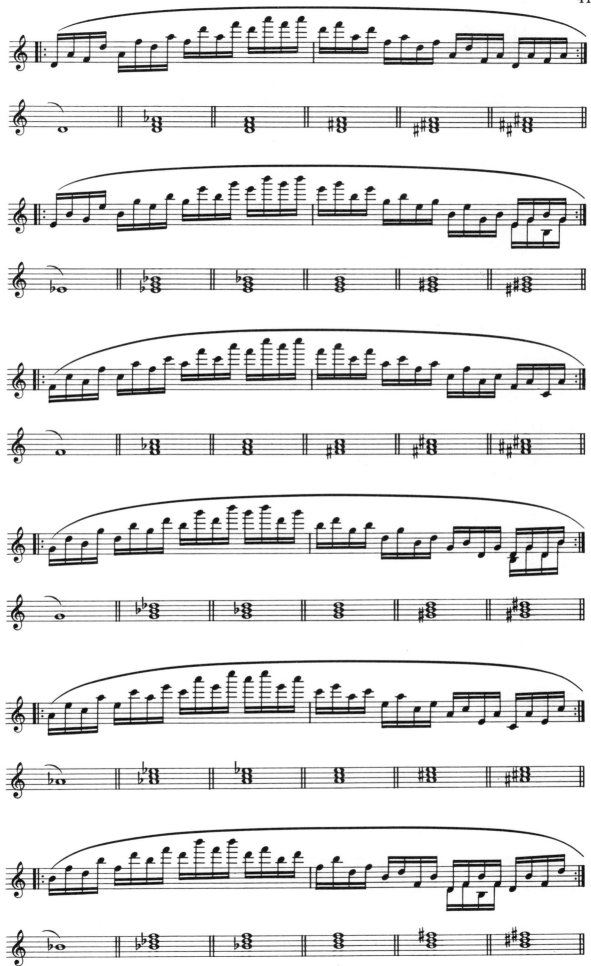

SECTION SIX – BROKEN ARPEGGIOS ON THE SEVENTH

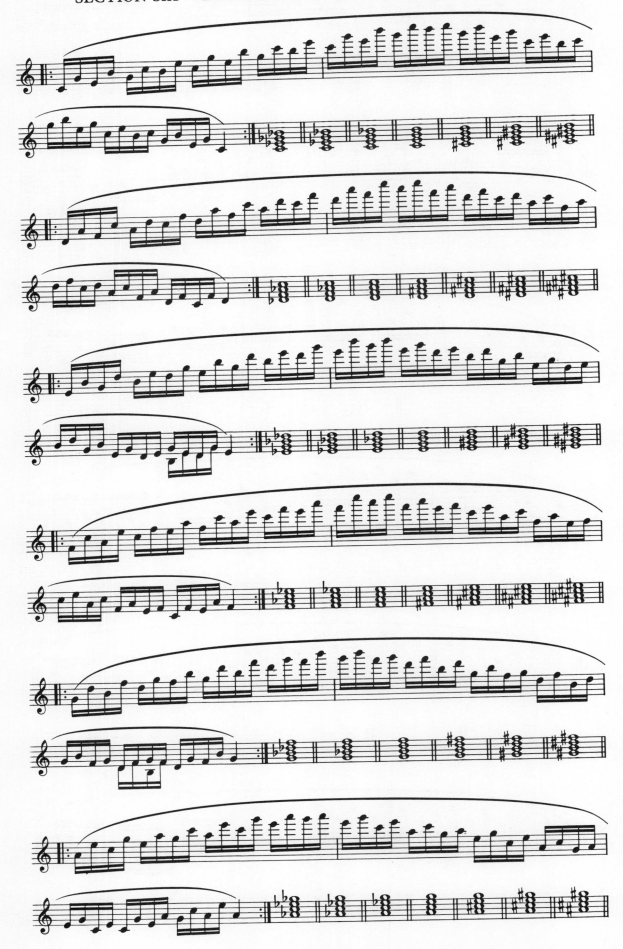

IMPROVISATION

Improvisation is the art of instantaneous musical invention, and generally means playing melodic patterns or melodies from a given series of chords, or from a bass line.

Improvisation is like talking without a script but talking about a *particular* subject.

Do you need a script when holding a conversation with someone? Of course not. You also don't need printed music to be able to make musical sounds. But to make sense of your musical sounds, you do need a subject on which to improvise.

The two most common forms of improvisation are jazz and baroque, or 18th century improvisation. Surprisingly, the two are very similar, as they are both based on the same chord progressions. It's the style which is different. This section will be concerned only with improvisation in the baroque and classical styles.

The studies are in approximate order of difficulty and start with simple exercises for chord and cadence recognition. Ideally, the keyboard part should be played to a group of performers (on any instruments) and repeated, without stopping, over and over again, each player having his turn at improvising. In this way, ideas are fed from one player to another.

Begin by freeing your mind from the printed page by playing as many 'variations' as you can on the three C's. Five examples are given. Try about twenty or thirty.

Before trying example (b), have you exhausted every possibility in your imagination? Different rhythms? Passing notes?

Examples: –

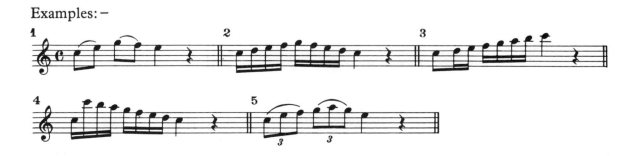

(b)

Examples:−

Exercise (c) gives a bass: put a cadence to it. Make several different cadences, some simple, some elaborate. Melodic examples are given which fit this bass.

(c)

Examples:−

Example (d) is a little longer and leads us on to the next stage.

(d)

(1) and (2) are examples of phrases from the flute repertoire. Study them. Either ask someone to play the basses repeatedly whilst you improvise to them, or, tape-record the bass repeatedly, and play to your own recording. Above the bass is what the composer originally wrote.

NOW, ON TO IMPROVISATION

There are some rules:–

In the beginning,

1 play anything that comes into your head. As you become bolder try to get a 'feel' for the harmonic movement of the bass line.

2 relax; there are no 'right' or 'wrong' notes; just notes in good or bad taste.

3 Quantz said – 'My advice is not to give yourself over too much to variations, but rather to apply yourself to playing a plain air nobly, truly, and clearly'. Don't therefore, go crazy and try to fit in as many notes as possible; rather, be economical and simple.

The basses are taken from the works of Telemann, Couperin, Vivaldi, Rameau, Handel and others. Chords have been added in the right hand part to make it easier to hear the harmonic progression of the bass. A good idea with a group of players is for the pianist to call out the names of the chords as he plays them and for the players to play *any* note of that chord. This quickly helps the players to get the 'feel' of the progressions.

Once the performers have understood the chordal progression, the right hand should be omitted, or just touched upon occasionally to assist with any particular difficulty.

Fit a tune or cadence to this bass. The chords are provided to assist you.

During the next few weeks, choose basses which appeal to you. Don't be too ambitious too soon. Do the easier ones first.

From now on, *don't* look at the right hand chords to help you improvise. Rather, keep the chord progression in your head.

Avoid following the direction of the bass line in your melody: contrary motion sounds best.

The sequences on page 33 of Volume 2 – TECHNIQUE should now be practised from memory, as should the Expressive Scales and Arpeggios in this book.

WHAT NOW?

You have, for sure, by now, a greater understanding of chordal progressions in 18th century music to the point where you are instantaneously *composing* music. Good eh?

Take some slow movements of Handel or Telemann sonatas. With your accompanist, improvise upon the melody either by changing it, as an exercise, or embellishing and decorating it. You must acquire 'good taste'. Read 'The Interpretation of Music' by Thurston Dart as a general introduction. Study Telemann's embellishments to his own slow movements in the 12 Methodische Sonaten, Op. XIII (Bärenreiter). These are very interesting.

Thereafter, the works of J. J. Quantz, C. P. E. Bach and the more recent works of Robert Donington will provide further study in greater depth.

PLAYING FROM MEMORY

All solo pianists and string players play from memory. Wind players sometimes do, but as there is no tradition of memorising concertos, they generally don't. This is a pity as musicians who do play from memory will confirm that it does ultimately lead to a greater freedom of expression in music.

Everyone can play from memory if their approach to it is right. You don't have to spend extra practice time on *acquiring* a 'memory'! *You have already got one.* It just needs exercising. Here are some tips:

1   Don't stare at the music all of the time like a rabbit at a snake. This applies to scales, exercises − in fact anything! Try walking away from the music stand. Look out of the window and continue the piece but don't fret if it goes wrong. You don't need a script to hold a conversation and you don't need music to play the flute.
2   Don't try too hard to be right. If you do slip up, it's hardly likely to start a nuclear war.

   Trying hard to 'get it right' is what stands in the way, most often, of a reliable memory.

   Enjoy the freedom of being without the restraint of a script. This may take time to understand but is well worth the effort.
3   Learn to improvise (see previous section). Learn to 'prelude'. In the 18/19th century, it was common to 'prelude' before playing a study or piece. This entailed playing a sort of cadenza in the same key as the piece but with freedom of rhythm and expression. You don't need to be told what to play: you only need the courage to try it.
4   Read page 33 of Practice Book No. 2. Include these sequences in your daily practice. Gradually learn to play them from memory.
5   Gradually accustom yourself to looking up from your copy whilst playing in public.

Printed and bound in Great Britain by
Halstan & Co. Ltd., Amersham, Bucks.   3/94 (17631)

TREVOR WYE

VIDEO

PLAY THE FLUTE
A beginner's guide

TUTORS

A BEGINNER'S BOOK FOR THE FLUTE
Part 1
Part 2
Piano Accompaniment

PRACTICE BOOKS FOR THE FLUTE
VOLUME 1 Tone
VOLUME 2 Technique
VOLUME 3 Articulation
VOLUME 4 Intonation and Vibrato
VOLUME 5 Breathing and Scales
VOLUME 6 Advanced Practice

A PICCOLO PRACTICE BOOK

PROPER FLUTE PLAYING

SOLO FLUTE

MUSIC FOR SOLO FLUTE

ARRANGEMENTS FOR FLUTE & PIANO

A COUPERIN ALBUM
AN ELGAR FLUTE ALBUM
A FAURE FLUTE ALBUM
A RAMEAU ALBUM
A SATIE FLUTE ALBUM
A SCHUMANN FLUTE ALBUM
A VIVALDI ALBUM

A FIRST LATIN-AMERICAN FLUTE ALBUM
A SECOND LATIN-AMERICAN FLUTE ALBUM

MOZART FLUTE CONCERTO IN G K.313
MOZART FLUTE CONCERTO IN D K.314 AND ANDANTE IN C K.315

SCHUBERT THEME AND VARIATIONS D 935 No. 3

FLUTE ENSEMBLE

THREE BRILLIANT SHOWPIECES

611 (91)